A book for the designer in every child and the child in every designer.

With thanks to Kim, George McIntosh, Greg Quinton, and Sam Hall.

thetypefaces.com
victionary.com

The Typefaces
Scott Lambert

For Avery, Belle, and Blythe,
my type of faces.

Ahhhhhhhh who is that,
in the black pointy hat?
Her yellow eyes, her cackle,
and her slightly **awkward** cat.

I'll **be** polite and I'll be charming,
I'll **back** away without alarming.

This martian makes mischief
of many other kinds.
He'll eat your bug **collection**
and **comb** your bear's behind.

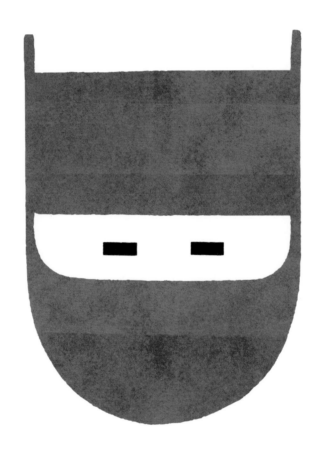

Dial your friends, email Gran,
and, if **danger** calls, find Batman.

A friendly bun is an **easy** one,
ears alert for fluffy fun.

If a typeface cannot be quiet,
we try not to give it attention.
So if you **find** one **freaking** out,
move on without a mention.

You can search over the under,
behind space and round the **ground**,
but **gee** you can't find someone
who just doesn't want to be found.

When you're done **huffy** stomping
and pulling stuff apart,
it's always good to remember
to **hug** a brand-new start.

Mistakes are how we learn,
don't go **invisible** and hide.
Have courage to try and try again,
trust your heart **inside**.

Who's this old gruffy,
all **jittery** and **jumpy**?
It's hard to make friends
with an animal so grumpy.

Just flip things around
to take away a frown.
Show the goat he's a **jolly**
elephant upside down.

The **king** of the alphabet
likes to **keep** the children hushed.
But we can't help but giggle
at his ridiculous moustache.

His trusty friend
is so proud and **loyal**,
and just loves the **legs**
of guests of royals.

Well, **Marvin** loves the show,
and the kids love Marvin Seal.
He'll promise not to splash and splish
in exchange for a fishy **meal**.

Ooooo you can never be sure
what the middle of the **night** might bring.
But this is just a book, you see,
there's really **no** such thing.

Keep your mind wide **open**,
for the real things that we know.
Observe some furry creatures,
who are nosing through the snow.

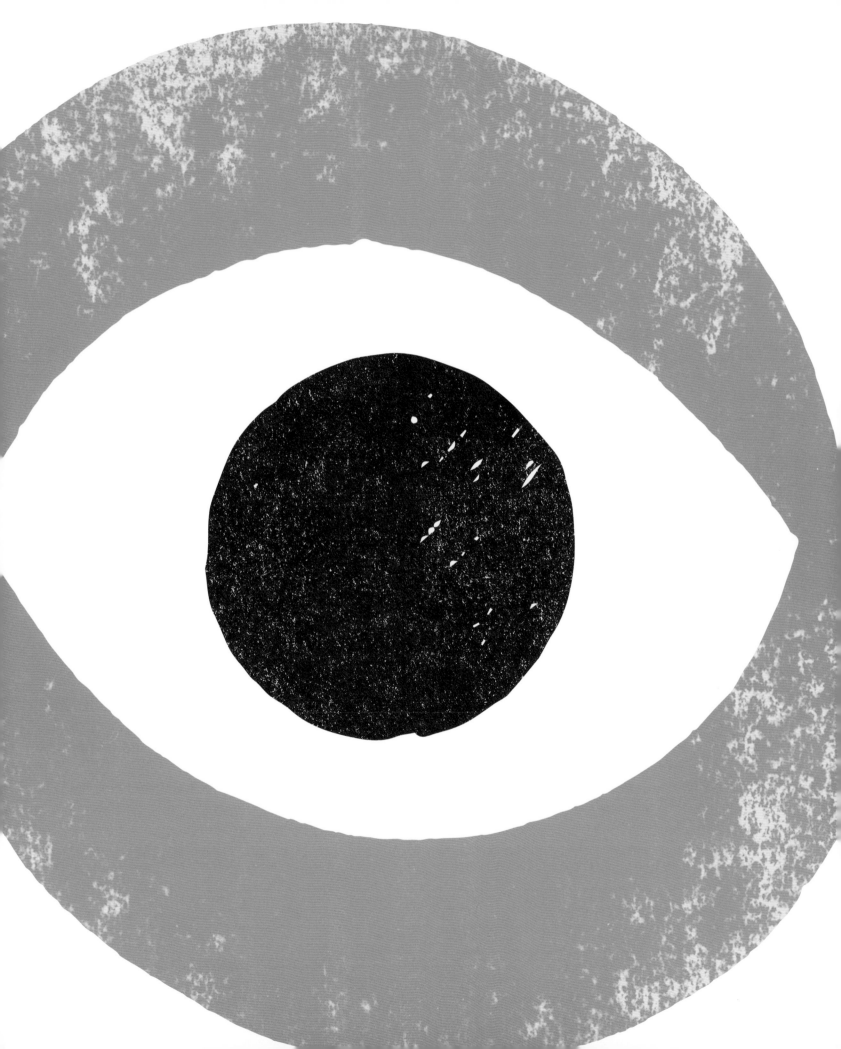

He has the **perfect** camouflage,
such splendid pure white hair.
But his nose is just a giveaway,
I see you **Poley** bear.

Quick, I see another,
a little one right there.
A mummy and her baby cub,
quite the happy pair.

Let's talk about it, **Rover**.
What happened to my lunch?
I do believe you woofed it down,
well, **really,** thanks a bunch.

We rarely **spot** Nessie
and I will tell you why.
Even though she is quite massive,
she's also a wee bit **shy**.

Now **twins** will always know
exactly how to **tease**.
Part of being bestest friends,
is being enemies.

I'll never forget when opposites met,
uh-oh you were hiding **under** the pages.
although I'm an elly, and you're a mouse
we can still be pals for ages.

My **voice** is rather squeaky
and my tail is creepy long,
but I'm really **very** friendly,
you'll love my cheesy song.

Hello and nice to meet you,
will you pop in for some tea?
Woooooah, no way, goodbye, I'm off!
You are not eating me.

It's tricky talking **xylophones**
to describe our next letter.
These mice won't forget, the best use yet,
is kisses, and they are much better. **xx**

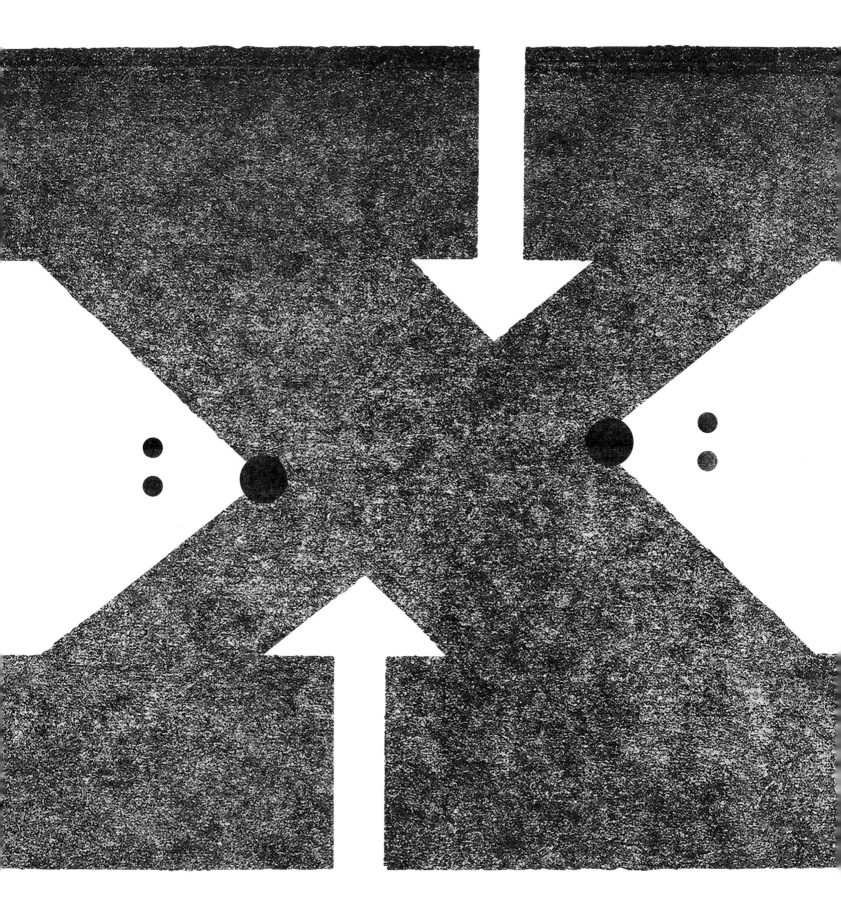

Why **yes** I rather like it,
our type sits pretty fine,
but I'm just beginning to wonder,
this tail, is it **yours** or mine?

And so we have **zipped** along
to **Zoe's** time on stage.
So clap and arf and clap some more
as they bow on the final page.

THE

Cover

T
Aldine Expanded.
William H Page.
1872

Y
Aldine Expanded.
William H Page.
1872

P
Mighty Slab.
Ryoichi Tsunekawa.
2016

E
Bodoni Classic Bold.
Giambattista Bodoni.
1798

The Typefaces

A
Aetna.
William H Page.
1820

B
Aldine Ornamented.
William H Page.
1872

C
Gothic Bold.
Hamilton
Manufacturing Co.
1840

D
Bodoni Classic Ultra.
Giambattista Bodoni.
1798

E
Gothic Bold.
Hamilton
Manufacturing Co.
1840

F
Gothic Bold.
Hamilton
Manufacturing Co.
1840

G
Aetna.
William H Page.
1820

H
Lexia Typographic Ad.
Dalton Maag.
2007

I
York Aldine.
William H Page.
1872

J
American Typewriter.
Joel Kaden,
Tony Stan.
1974

K
ITC Barcelona.
Edward Benguiat.
1981

L
Aldine Ornamented.
William H Page.
1870

M
Bradley.
William H Bradley.
1894

N
Initials Gothic C.
Henric Pieterszoon.
1768

O
Lydian.
Warren Chappell.
1938

P
Bradley.
William H Bradley.
1894

Q
York Aldine.
William H Page.
1872

R
Aldine Expanded.
William H Page.
1872

S
Atlas.
Day & Collins.
1904

T
Aldine Expanded.
William H Page.
1872

U
Colette.
Greg Lindy.
2012

V
Murga.
Angel Koziupa,
Alejandro Paul.
2003

W
De Little.
Robert D De Little.
1892

X
Ziggurat.
Jonathan Hoefler.
1991

Y
Aldine Expanded.
William H Page.
1872

Z
Ziggurat Black Italic.
Jonathan Hoefler.
1991

Endpapers

C
Bodoni Classic Ultra.
Giambattista Bodoni.
1798

Rhymes

The pages are set in
Akzidenz Grotesk Pro,
originally designed by
Herman Berthold
in 1896.

©2019 viction:workshop ltd.
Published by viction:workshop ltd.

**VICTION
VICTION**

Unit C, 7th Floor, Seabright Plaza,
9-23 Shell Street, North Point, Hong Kong
URL: www.victionary.com   Email: we@victionary.com
📘 @victionworkshop
🐦 @victionary_
📷 @victionworkshop

Illustration & design © Scott Lambert 2019
Text © Scott Lambert 2019
URL: www.design-positive.com

ISBN 978-988-79034-0-6

Printed and bound in China